# Weekly Planner
# and **Organizer**

## for the
## Work-at-Home Mom

Activinotes

## *Activinotes*

DAILY JOURNALS, PLANNERS, NOTEBOOKS AND OTHER BLANK BOOKS

# Weekly Planner

| MONDAY | TUESDAY | WEDNESDAY | THURSDAY |
|--------|---------|-----------|----------|
|        |         |           |          |
|        |         |           |          |

| FRIDAY | SATURDAY | SUNDAY | To Do List |
|--------|----------|--------|------------|
|        |          |        |            |
|        |          |        |            |

*Notes :*

| To Do | Reminder | To Buy |
|-------|----------|--------|
|       |          |        |

# Journal

# Weekly Planner

| MONDAY | TUESDAY | WEDNESDAY | THURSDAY |
|---|---|---|---|
| | | | |
| | | | |

| FRIDAY | SATURDAY | SUNDAY | To Do List |
|---|---|---|---|
| | | | |
| | | | |

Notes :

The Best Mom

| To Do | Reminder | To Buy |
|-------|----------|--------|
|       |          |        |

# Journal

_____
_____
_____
_____
_____
_____
_____
_____
_____
_____
_____
_____
_____
_____
_____
_____
_____

# Weekly Planner

| MONDAY | TUESDAY | WEDNESDAY | THURSDAY |
|--------|---------|-----------|----------|
|        |         |           |          |
|        |         |           |          |

| FRIDAY | SATURDAY | SUNDAY | To Do List |
|--------|----------|--------|-----------|
|        |          |        |           |
|        |          |        |           |

Notes :

| To Do | Reminder | To Buy |
|---|---|---|
|  |  |  |

# Journal

# Weekly Planner

| MONDAY | TUESDAY | WEDNESDAY | THURSDAY |
|--------|---------|-----------|----------|
|        |         |           |          |
|        |         |           |          |

| FRIDAY | SATURDAY | SUNDAY | To Do List |
|--------|----------|--------|------------|
|        |          |        |            |
|        |          |        |            |

Notes :

Work at Home Mom

The Best Mom

ORIGINAL

| To Do | Reminder | To Buy |
| --- | --- | --- |
| | | |

# Journal

_____
_____
_____
_____
_____
_____
_____
_____
_____
_____
_____
_____
_____
_____
_____
_____
_____
_____

# Weekly Planner

| MONDAY | TUESDAY | WEDNESDAY | THURSDAY |
|--------|---------|-----------|----------|
|  |  |  |  |
|  |  |  |  |

| FRIDAY | SATURDAY | SUNDAY | To Do List |
|--------|----------|--------|-----------|
|  |  |  |  |
|  |  |  |  |

Notes :

The Best Mom
ORIGINAL

| To Do | Reminder | To Buy |
|-------|----------|--------|
|       |          |        |

# Journal

_____
_____
_____
_____
_____
_____
_____
_____
_____
_____
_____
_____
_____
_____
_____
_____

# Weekly Planner

| MONDAY | TUESDAY | WEDNESDAY | THURSDAY |
|--------|---------|-----------|----------|
|        |         |           |          |
|        |         |           |          |

| FRIDAY | SATURDAY | SUNDAY | To Do List |
|--------|----------|--------|------------|
|        |          |        |            |
|        |          |        |            |

Notes :

| To Do | Reminder | To Buy |
|---|---|---|
|  |  |  |

# Journal

# Weekly Planner

| MONDAY | TUESDAY | WEDNESDAY | THURSDAY |
|--------|---------|-----------|----------|
|        |         |           |          |
|        |         |           |          |

| FRIDAY | SATURDAY | SUNDAY | To Do List |
|--------|----------|--------|------------|
|        |          |        |            |
|        |          |        |            |

Notes :

| To Do | Reminder | To Buy |
|-------|----------|--------|
|       |          |        |

# Journal

# Weekly Planner

| MONDAY | TUESDAY | WEDNESDAY | THURSDAY |
|--------|---------|-----------|----------|
|        |         |           |          |
|        |         |           |          |

| FRIDAY | SATURDAY | SUNDAY | To Do List |
|--------|----------|--------|------------|
|        |          |        |            |
|        |          |        |            |

Notes :

| To Do | Reminder | To Buy |
| --- | --- | --- |
| | | |

# Journal

# Weekly Planner

| MONDAY | TUESDAY | WEDNESDAY | THURSDAY |
|---|---|---|---|
| | | | |
| | | | |

| FRIDAY | SATURDAY | SUNDAY | To Do List |
|---|---|---|---|
| | | | |
| | | | |

Notes:

The Best Mom
ORIGINAL

| To Do | Reminder | To Buy |
|-------|----------|--------|
|       |          |        |

# Journal

_____
_____
_____
_____
_____
_____
_____
_____
_____
_____
_____
_____
_____
_____
_____
_____
_____
_____

# Weekly Planner

| MONDAY | TUESDAY | WEDNESDAY | THURSDAY |
|--------|---------|-----------|----------|
|        |         |           |          |
|        |         |           |          |

| FRIDAY | SATURDAY | SUNDAY | To Do List |
|--------|----------|--------|------------|
|        |          |        |            |
|        |          |        |            |

*Notes :*

The Best Mom

| To Do | Reminder | To Buy |
|-------|----------|--------|
|       |          |        |

# Journal

# Weekly Planner

| MONDAY | TUESDAY | WEDNESDAY | THURSDAY |
|--------|---------|-----------|----------|
|        |         |           |          |
|        |         |           |          |

| FRIDAY | SATURDAY | SUNDAY | To Do List |
|--------|----------|--------|------------|
|        |          |        |            |
|        |          |        |            |

Notes :

| To Do | Reminder | To Buy |
|-------|----------|--------|
|       |          |        |

# Journal

# Weekly Planner

| MONDAY | TUESDAY | WEDNESDAY | THURSDAY |
|--------|---------|-----------|----------|
|        |         |           |          |
|        |         |           |          |

| FRIDAY | SATURDAY | SUNDAY | To Do List |
|--------|----------|--------|------------|
|        |          |        |            |
|        |          |        |            |

Notes :

| To Do | Reminder | To Buy |
|---|---|---|
| | | |

# Journal

---

---

---

---

---

---

---

---

---

---

---

---

---

---

---

---

---

---

---

---

The Best Mom

# Weekly Planner

| MONDAY | TUESDAY | WEDNESDAY | THURSDAY |
|--------|---------|-----------|----------|
|        |         |           |          |
|        |         |           |          |

| FRIDAY | SATURDAY | SUNDAY | To Do List |
|--------|----------|--------|------------|
|        |          |        |            |
|        |          |        |            |

Notes :

| To Do | Reminder | To Buy |
|-------|----------|--------|
|       |          |        |

# Journal

# Weekly Planner

| MONDAY | TUESDAY | WEDNESDAY | THURSDAY |
|--------|---------|-----------|----------|
|        |         |           |          |
|        |         |           |          |

| FRIDAY | SATURDAY | SUNDAY | To Do List |
|--------|----------|--------|------------|
|        |          |        |            |
|        |          |        |            |

Notes :

| To Do | Reminder | To Buy |
|-------|----------|--------|
|       |          |        |

# Journal

_____
_____
_____
_____
_____
_____
_____
_____
_____
_____
_____
_____
_____
_____
_____
_____
_____
_____
_____
_____

# Weekly Planner

| MONDAY | TUESDAY | WEDNESDAY | THURSDAY |
|---|---|---|---|
|  |  |  |  |
|  |  |  |  |

| FRIDAY | SATURDAY | SUNDAY | To Do List |
|---|---|---|---|
|  |  |  |  |
|  |  |  |  |

Notes :

| To Do | Reminder | To Buy |
|-------|----------|--------|
|       |          |        |

# Journal

# Weekly Planner

| MONDAY | TUESDAY | WEDNESDAY | THURSDAY |
|--------|---------|-----------|----------|
|        |         |           |          |
|        |         |           |          |

| FRIDAY | SATURDAY | SUNDAY | To Do List |
|--------|----------|--------|------------|
|        |          |        |            |
|        |          |        |            |

Notes:

| To Do | Reminder | To Buy |
|-------|----------|--------|
|       |          |        |

# Journal

# Weekly Planner

| MONDAY | TUESDAY | WEDNESDAY | THURSDAY |
|--------|---------|-----------|----------|
|  |  |  |  |
|  |  |  |  |

| FRIDAY | SATURDAY | SUNDAY | To Do List |
|--------|----------|--------|------------|
|  |  |  |  |
|  |  |  |  |

Notes :

| To Do | Reminder | To Buy |
|-------|----------|--------|
|       |          |        |

# Journal

_____
_____
_____
_____
_____
_____
_____
_____
_____
_____
_____
_____
_____
_____
_____
_____
_____
_____

# Weekly Planner

| MONDAY | TUESDAY | WEDNESDAY | THURSDAY |
|--------|---------|-----------|----------|
|        |         |           |          |
|        |         |           |          |

| FRIDAY | SATURDAY | SUNDAY | To Do List |
|--------|----------|--------|------------|
|        |          |        |            |
|        |          |        |            |

Notes :

| To Do | Reminder | To Buy |
|---|---|---|
| | | |

# Journal

# Weekly Planner

| MONDAY | TUESDAY | WEDNESDAY | THURSDAY |
|--------|---------|-----------|----------|
|        |         |           |          |
|        |         |           |          |

| FRIDAY | SATURDAY | SUNDAY | To Do List |
|--------|----------|--------|------------|
|        |          |        |            |
|        |          |        |            |

Notes :

The Best Mom

| To Do | Reminder | To Buy |
|---|---|---|
|  |  |  |

# Journal

# Weekly Planner

| MONDAY | TUESDAY | WEDNESDAY | THURSDAY |
|--------|---------|-----------|----------|
|        |         |           |          |
|        |         |           |          |

| FRIDAY | SATURDAY | SUNDAY | To Do List |
|--------|----------|--------|------------|
|        |          |        |            |
|        |          |        |            |

Notes :

| To Do | Reminder | To Buy |
|-------|----------|--------|
|       |          |        |

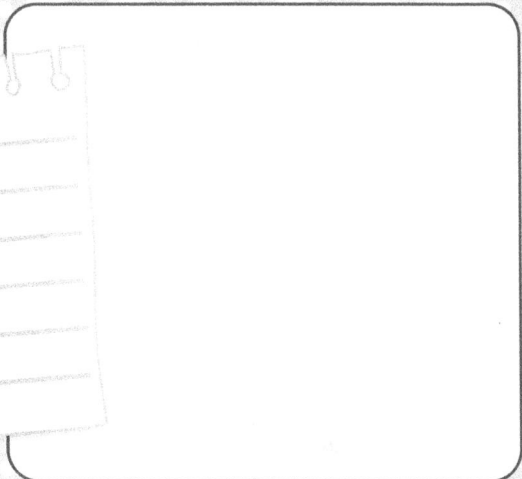

# Journal

_____
_____
_____
_____
_____
_____
_____
_____
_____
_____
_____
_____
_____
_____
_____
_____
_____
_____

# Weekly Planner

| MONDAY | TUESDAY | WEDNESDAY | THURSDAY |
|--------|---------|-----------|----------|
|        |         |           |          |
|        |         |           |          |

| FRIDAY | SATURDAY | SUNDAY | To Do List |
|--------|----------|--------|------------|
|        |          |        |            |
|        |          |        |            |

Notes :

| To Do | Reminder | To Buy |
|-------|----------|--------|
|       |          |        |

# Journal

# Weekly Planner

| MONDAY | TUESDAY | WEDNESDAY | THURSDAY |
|--------|---------|-----------|----------|
|        |         |           |          |
|        |         |           |          |

| FRIDAY | SATURDAY | SUNDAY | To Do List |
|--------|----------|--------|------------|
|        |          |        |            |
|        |          |        |            |

Notes :

| To Do | Reminder | To Buy |
|-------|----------|--------|
|       |          |        |

# Journal

The Best Mom

# Weekly Planner

| MONDAY | TUESDAY | WEDNESDAY | THURSDAY |
|--------|---------|-----------|----------|
|        |         |           |          |
|        |         |           |          |

| FRIDAY | SATURDAY | SUNDAY | To Do List |
|--------|----------|--------|------------|
|        |          |        |            |
|        |          |        |            |

Notes :

| To Do | Reminder | To Buy |
|-------|----------|--------|
|       |          |        |

# Journal

# Weekly Planner

| MONDAY | TUESDAY | WEDNESDAY | THURSDAY |
|--------|---------|-----------|----------|
|        |         |           |          |
|        |         |           |          |

| FRIDAY | SATURDAY | SUNDAY | To Do List |
|--------|----------|--------|------------|
|        |          |        |            |
|        |          |        |            |

Notes :

| To Do | Reminder | To Buy |
|---|---|---|
|  |  |  |

# Journal

# Weekly Planner

| MONDAY | TUESDAY | WEDNESDAY | THURSDAY |
|---|---|---|---|
|  |  |  |  |
|  |  |  |  |

| FRIDAY | SATURDAY | SUNDAY | To Do List |
|---|---|---|---|
|  |  |  |  |
|  |  |  |  |

Notes :

| To Do | Reminder | To Buy |
|-------|----------|--------|
|       |          |        |

# Journal

---------------------------------------------

---------------------------------------------

---------------------------------------------

---------------------------------------------

---------------------------------------------

---------------------------------------------

---------------------------------------------

---------------------------------------------

---------------------------------------------

---------------------------------------------

---------------------------------------------

---------------------------------------------

---------------------------------------------

---------------------------------------------

---------------------------------------------

---------------------------------------------

---------------------------------------------

---------------------------------------------

---------------------------------------------

# Weekly Planner

| MONDAY | TUESDAY | WEDNESDAY | THURSDAY |
|---|---|---|---|
| | | | |
| | | | |

| FRIDAY | SATURDAY | SUNDAY | To Do List |
|---|---|---|---|
| | | | |
| | | | |

Notes:

The Best Mom
ORIGINAL

| To Do | Reminder | To Buy |
|-------|----------|--------|
|       |          |        |

# Journal

_____
_____
_____
_____
_____
_____
_____
_____
_____
_____
_____
_____
_____
_____
_____
_____
_____
_____
_____
_____
_____

# Weekly Planner

| MONDAY | TUESDAY | WEDNESDAY | THURSDAY |
|---|---|---|---|
| | | | |
| | | | |

| FRIDAY | SATURDAY | SUNDAY | To Do List |
|---|---|---|---|
| | | | |
| | | | |

Notes:

The Best Mom
ORIGINAL

| To Do | Reminder | To Buy |
|-------|----------|--------|
|       |          |        |

# Journal

# Weekly Planner

| MONDAY | TUESDAY | WEDNESDAY | THURSDAY |
|--------|---------|-----------|----------|
|        |         |           |          |
|        |         |           |          |

| FRIDAY | SATURDAY | SUNDAY | To Do List |
|--------|----------|--------|------------|
|        |          |        |            |
|        |          |        |            |

Notes :

| To Do | Reminder | To Buy |
|-------|----------|--------|
|       |          |        |

# Journal

# Weekly Planner

| MONDAY | TUESDAY | WEDNESDAY | THURSDAY |
|---|---|---|---|
|  |  |  |  |
|  |  |  |  |

| FRIDAY | SATURDAY | SUNDAY | To Do List |
|---|---|---|---|
|  |  |  |  |
|  |  |  |  |

Notes :

The Best Mom
ORIGINAL

| To Do | Reminder | To Buy |
|-------|----------|--------|
|       |          |        |

# Journal

# Weekly Planner

| MONDAY | TUESDAY | WEDNESDAY | THURSDAY |
|--------|---------|-----------|----------|
|        |         |           |          |
|        |         |           |          |

| FRIDAY | SATURDAY | SUNDAY | To Do List |
|--------|----------|--------|------------|
|        |          |        |            |
|        |          |        |            |

*Notes:*

| To Do | Reminder | To Buy |
|-------|----------|--------|
|       |          |        |

# Journal

_____
_____
_____
_____
_____
_____
_____
_____
_____
_____
_____
_____
_____
_____
_____
_____
_____
_____
_____
_____

# Weekly Planner

| MONDAY | TUESDAY | WEDNESDAY | THURSDAY |
|---|---|---|---|
|  |  |  |  |
|  |  |  |  |

| FRIDAY | SATURDAY | SUNDAY | To Do List |
|---|---|---|---|
|  |  |  |  |
|  |  |  |  |

Notes :

| To Do | Reminder | To Buy |
| --- | --- | --- |
| | | |

# Journal

# Weekly Planner

| MONDAY | TUESDAY | WEDNESDAY | THURSDAY |
|--------|---------|-----------|----------|
|        |         |           |          |
|        |         |           |          |

| FRIDAY | SATURDAY | SUNDAY | To Do List |
|--------|----------|--------|------------|
|        |          |        |            |
|        |          |        |            |

Notes :

| To Do | Reminder | To Buy |
|-------|----------|--------|
|       |          |        |

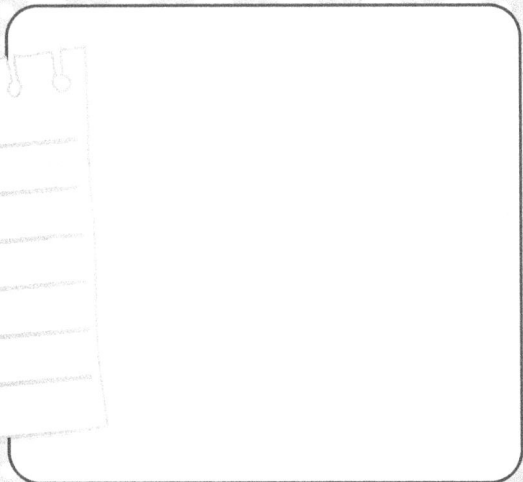

# Journal

# Weekly Planner

| MONDAY | TUESDAY | WEDNESDAY | THURSDAY |
|---|---|---|---|
| | | | |
| | | | |

| FRIDAY | SATURDAY | SUNDAY | To Do List |
|---|---|---|---|
| | | | |
| | | | |

*Notes :*

| To Do | Reminder | To Buy |
|-------|----------|--------|
|       |          |        |

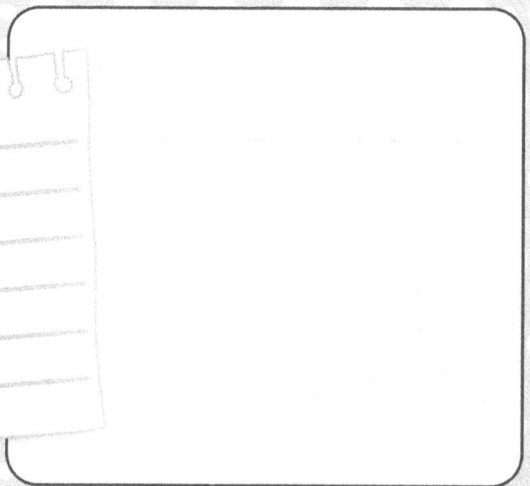

# Journal

---
---
---
---
---
---
---
---
---
---
---
---
---
---
---
---
---
---
---

# Weekly Planner

| MONDAY | TUESDAY | WEDNESDAY | THURSDAY |
|--------|---------|-----------|----------|
|        |         |           |          |
|        |         |           |          |

| FRIDAY | SATURDAY | SUNDAY | To Do List |
|--------|----------|--------|-----------|
|        |          |        |           |
|        |          |        |           |

Notes:

| To Do | Reminder | To Buy |
|---|---|---|
| | | |

# Journal

# Notes

www.ingramcontent.com/pod-product-compliance
Lightning Source LLC
Chambersburg PA
CBHW081338090426
42737CB00017B/3202